Another Way

Another Way

Also by Dale Turner and available from High Tide Press:

Different Seasons: Twelve Months of Wisdom & Inspiration

Grateful Living

DALE TURNER

Another Way

Open-Minded Faithfulness

HIGH TIDE PRESS
HOMEWOOD, ILLINOIS

A High Tide Book

Published by High Tide Press Inc.

3650 West 183rd Street, Homewood, Illinois 60430

Copyright © 2001 by Dale E. Turner

Turner, Rev. Dale E. Another Way / by Dale Turner — 2nd ed.

ISBN 1-892696-22-3

Printed in the United States of America

Book design by Alex Lubertozzi and Diane J. Bell

Second Edition

For ordering information call (888) 231-7229

Printed on acid-free paper.

To Ruth H. Williamson–Kirkland,
my faithful and tireless assistant
whose loving and persistent efforts
have helped turn concept into reality.

Table of Contents

Foreword

Since 1997, High Tide Press has published the works of Dr. Dale Turner. We were proud to travel with Dr. Turner on his writing journey from newspaper columnist to author.

I admire how Rev. Turner's ministry, his actions and his words have made him a role model to thousands. He has been called "a remarkable spiritual and civic leader," and his thoughts and ideas appeal to people from many walks of life and from numerous different faiths.

His immensely popular debut, *Different Seasons: Twelve Months of Wisdom and Inspiration* sold out of its first printing. Encouraged by the popularity of *Different Seasons*, we welcomed his second book, *Grateful Living*, in 1998. While *Different Seasons* offers an inspirational tour of the year, *Grateful Living* is a collection of stories on faith, activism, love, grief, forgiveness and humor.

Another Way: Open-Minded Faithfulness is a collection of statements that express the breadth and depth of Dr. Turner's ministry to mankind. While there are many books of quotes, *Another Way* is uniquely the work of one man. The statements are taken from the more than 1,000 columns written by Dr. Turner for the *Seattle Times*.

I continue to be amazed at his ability to express

profoundly meaningful concepts in simple, moving prose. I believe that you, the reader will more than enjoy this book; your life will be enriched. As you contemplate Dr. Turner's thoughts on Reassurance, Faith, Community, Triumphant Living, Love, and Reaching Out, I hope you will become a stronger and better person in each of those areas. I know I have.

—Art Dykstra
Editor-in-Chief
High Tide Press

Preface

As a young divinity student I arrived at Yale with a box full of books, a brand new four-drawer file cabinet, and a very literal interpretation of the Bible. I did not enter the ministry because I thought I had all the answers or had arrived at any spiritual fulfillment, but because I wanted to spend my life surrounded by others who were continually searching for God and His loving relationship to each of us.

As I proceeded with my education, my literal views of the Bible were challenged, stretched, tweaked and scrutinized. I remember standing in one class holding my Bible and challenging a professor who disagreed with my more legalistic views on how the Bible should be understood. Remembering this fills me with some chagrin, but also with the knowledge that from the very beginning, I was working hard to develop my own beliefs and relationship to God. And, I was willing to stand up and be counted for what I cherished.

As my years in seminary proceeded, I developed what would be the foundation for my relationship with God and the touchstone of my ministry. It was no longer a simplistic view of God as seen through a literal translation of the Bible, but what would, since my Yale Divinity School graduation in 1943, lead me through two long pastorates and nearly 20 years of writing as the religion columnist for the Seattle Times. This foundation would be the framework for one of the many ways of defining life as a Christian. It would be, Another Way.

This divinity school groundwork of beliefs would continue to be honed, questioned and refined in the front lines of my daily life, in my work as a minister, husband, father and friend. I strove for a set of beliefs that would combine open-mindedness, that makes for progress, with a loyalty to those convictions that conserve the best contributions of the past. These views would be born and reborn again. As I struggled with applying the principles that I felt were most representative of Christ's life and message for humankind to the thorny and complicated issues of our day—peace, minority and women's rights, homosexuality, euthanasia, abortion, multi-faith cooperation and more. It would stand with me as I dealt also with the myriad of age-old problems that affect all humans—grief, loneliness, disability, disappointment, temptation, evil, misfortune, prejudice and sin.

I began to believe more and more that religious exclusiveness and blind patriotism were enemies of the God who created us all. They are a common ailment of our day, a premature formation of religious opinion. Many people seem to start out intent on discovering the world of truth, but then settle down on the first little island of knowledge, build a fortress, then shoot down any idea that threatens their security. Instead, I came to believe that although I can know God within the confines of my own Christian community, I can only know part of God. It appears that we must all learn to live with the mystery and ambiguity of life with an infinite God, because we have only our finite minds. Many questions will remain unanswered on this side of life.

However, my belief became more firm: Christ teaches us that God's love is as international as the sun that shines on the just and the unjust alike. We are all God's children. The Creator desires a loving relationship with each of his children. God has a purpose for each individual, and no gift of mind or spirit is so small or so useless that it cannot be turned to a constructive end.

However, it is not enough simply to believe in God. It is our commitment to the Creator's will that gives integrity to our faith. Religion is behavior and not mere belief. Therefore we become worthy of God's gifts to us and trust in us when we commit our lives to the Creator's way of unconditional, non-manipulative and all-accepting love. It is this spirit of love, and acceptance of diversity that must be nurtured. Such a spirit—tolerant, gracious and charitable—offers a basis for happy and harmonious community life. Barriers that separate people must be fashioned into bridges. Enemies must become friends. Life's highest service is performed by those who love and encourage the good and the love in others. Jesus declared flatly, everything opposed to love, justice and brotherhood, is doomed. This is because at the center of the universe is a God of loving purpose for all people. Jesus was a kind and loving friend to all. He never met an unimportant person. He wrapped the blanket of compassion around the poor and the dispossessed. People came to Him with their burdens and left with a new and vital faith in themselves and in God.

For this reason, I have centered my life and my

ministry around the principle that "The greatest gift we can give to the Heavenly Father is to do something for one of His other children."

This is the essence of Another Way. I do not believe that I, or anyone else, has all the answers. A God small enough to be fully understood would not be big enough to meet our needs. But we do not have to understand the whole of God to believe in God. It is a mark of spiritual growth to have questions. Even after conscientious study, it is no disgrace to feel that we do not have all the answers. It is our Creator's intention that we not only go through life, but that we grow through life, continuously in search of more light, truth and love.

As I have questioned, doubted and searched for answers, for a right relationship with God and with my brothers and sisters, my way has been to attempt to live and to preach God's love. My belief is that the deepest need of the human spirit is community—common unity—good will, love and acceptance. The most human thing we have to do in life is to learn to speak our honest convictions and feelings and live with the consequences. This is the first requirement of love and it makes us vulnerable to others who may ridicule us. But it is important to be able to give our vulnerability to others. I am humbled by my attempts to honestly and openly speak my convictions, live with the consequences, and continuously attempt to extend my hand in friendship and love to those who may not agree with me.

Ours is a complex and often puzzling day, but the simplicities of love and caring must come center stage. Everywhere in our society people are bleeding to death spiritually and emotionally. The tourniquet of love and caring must be applied. The good life is marked by countless little extra deeds of love and helpfulness done throughout each day. When we extend ourselves and do the extras that are open to us, we make the world a brighter, better and more loving place in which to live.

Love is the active power which enables us to break through walls that separate us—the doorway through which the human spirit moves from solitude to society, and from selfishness to service. Let us extend the hand of love to one another and take part as co-creators of our world with the Creator of us all.

Reassurance

With our finite and limited minds we cannot be expected to grasp all the mysteries of an infinite universe or know the whole of God's plan. We will never "arrive." The wisest people are those who, although unrelenting in their quest for answers, trustingly leave some of the problems in the hands of God who knows the whole. There will be times when God's felt presence will elude us. There will be times when we cannot achieve what we set out to do, when we fall short of our hopes and goals, when life's problems and trials stop us in our tracks.

However, there is no dishonor in imperfection. The dishonor lies in not turning to full account whatever possibilities do exist. Thankfully, we do not have to be perfect to make positive contributions to life. God does not wait for the world's work to be done by perfect people. The Creator only asks that with faith we proceed to follow His path of love and service to all.

appily, we do not move into the future alone. No matter what our need, there will usually be someone near to lend a hand. We live and move and have our being in God's presence. We are not orphans in an empty world.

+∿+

No one needs to let his or her limitations define the whole of his or her life.

+∿+

There are reassurances in the midst
of fragmented days. A consciousness
of incompleteness is essential to a rational
view of life as a whole.
The real is always a fragment of the ideal.
The greater one's ideal,
the more fragmentary the real sometimes
appears. And the more we try to do, or the
better we try to become,
the greater will be our consciousness
of fragmentation and incompleteness.

There is nothing more certain than uncertainty.

✦

In spite of the complexities of our fast moving
society, it is still possible to hear that still, small voice
of conscience and to catch hold
of what is honest and true.

✦

The experiences of many human beings has revealed
that trouble, while appearing as an unwelcome
intruder, may be a blessing in disguise.
Often, it is not at the hour of trouble, but only
in retrospect, that we see the positive values of the
problems we have encountered, and the hand
of God's leading. There are no such things
as hard knocks without advantages.

✦

When we believe that the days ahead will be good days,
we move forward with confidence and hope,
and by such positive outlook,
we help to fulfill our expectations.

✦

Others find it easier to relate to us
when they see us fail, make mistakes and experience
disappointment; our humanness is revealed.
We must learn to see each handicap in larger
perspective and not magnify it out of proportion
to what ought to be its inhibiting power.

God has a purpose for each individual,
and no gift of mind or spirit is so small or useless
that it cannot be turned to a constructive end.

✦

It is reassuring to know that a person does not
have to be a star to be useful. Giving the support
that enables another to succeed is one of the finest
expressions of humility, love and unselfishness.

✦

Often those who serve in supportive roles
go unheralded, but without them others would not
succeed. Most of us will never be famous
or widely known, but it is heartening to know
that no one is useless who encourages and enables
others to realize their best.

✦

Only our relationship to God can ultimately rescue
us from our loneliness. We are not alone.

✦

Much of life is larger than we are and was never
intended to be finished.
It is open-ended and ongoing.

✦

Fragmentism is not only inevitable but may have its
essential place in the completed whole. Life is not
made up of one piece, but of many pieces.

I never cease to be lifted in spirit
by those who stay with it, even though things
are not what they wished they would be.

+∿+

The world's work does not wait
to be done by perfect people.

+∿+

When we accept the fact that much of life is hard,
it somehow becomes amazingly easier—easier for us,
and for those around us
who are spared our complaints.

+∿+

We do not know what each new day will bring,
for God does not permit us to see over the hills
or around the corners. For some, the uncertainty
of the future brings fear and apprehension.
The best answer for them is the realization
that the future comes one day at a time.

+∿+

A failure may be a blessing in disguise. It may mean
self-discovery or a new direction for life.

+∿+

A failure simply reveals that something has been
tried. If we have tried to do something and failed,
we are vastly better off than having tried
to do nothing and succeeded.

God may not will all that comes to us in the days
ahead, but He will be present to uphold us
and sustain us in whatever experience
will be ours of joy or sorrow.

†∾†

Some of life's deepest insights and larger truths are
ushered into our lives by pain and sorrow. Again and
again, we come to see that great lives sing most gloriously when assaulted by the winds of adversity.

†∾†

To see life as given to us by a loving God
is to know that life is invested with deathless meaning
and invincible dignity.

†∾†

It should be liberating to know that we do not
have to know everything. Half of being smart
is knowing what we do not know.

†∾†

The hard truth is that we have no right to happiness,
per se. Life carries no such warranty. Those who set
out to pursue happiness seldom find it. For happiness is not a product to be found
but a byproduct of the search.

†∾†

Truth never needs to fear the light.

The biggest disservice to ourselves and to others
is to have a good impulse to commend someone,
and then, to remain silent.

꒦꒷꒦

Suffering and sorrow remain the supreme
mystery of life. A great source of steadiness
can be found in the knowledge that countless others
have faced precisely the same problems without being
utterly defeated in spirit. No wound of the body or
soul is unique or entirely new, and others
with similar scars have something to say to us.
Among the sources of human strength is a resource
unequaled—the friendship of any person who has
preceded another through a similar valley
who can quietly say, "I understand."

꒦꒷꒦

Our days are as the shadows that fly across the sunny
hill. The years pass swiftly. This can be a call
to give priority to values of worth in the brief days
allotted to us. Death is a part of life,
and is not devoid of positive contributions;
the presence of death
makes more meaningful all of the values of life.

꒦꒷꒦

So many of the tragedies of life seem meaningless
and unnecessary. Yet with the responsible use of the
brain the Creator gave us, we come to conclusions
that enable us to believe in the rationality
of the world and the love and goodness of God.

We may not be able to take away
another person's grief and pain, but we may share it.

❧

Heaven begins on earth for those who are unselfish
and caring, who live with a consciousness
of God's continuing presence. Eternal life is not a
postponed affair that comes after death. It is a way of
living in this world that says that life is endless
and unconquerable.

❧

The good news of the Gospel is that the club is still
open to membership. It is not a private, exclusive
group. "Whoever will, may come."

❧

You are a factor in every situation.
Never discount your own importance in the struggle
to make a better world. We may never occupy
positions of high importance nor directly influence
dramatic decisions, but if we are faithful with what we
have, where we are, there will never come an end
to the good that we have done.

❧

Grief, like trouble, is never
welcome, but once it comes it can be
transmuted and channeled into service and sympathy,
into understanding and undergirding of others.
In all things, God can work for good.

There are possibilities for creative and constructive
replenishment of body, mind and spirit
when we listen; when we are still
we stand the chance of learning something.

✢

Life is not all velvet. Some of it is sandpaper.
God puts thorns on rose bushes.

✢

God gave us a backbone to bear our ills,
but God gave us a funny bone, as well.

✢

One of the most perplexing and frustrating aspects
of life is the sense of incompleteness
and fragmentalism that characterizes
many of our days. There is hope, however,
when we realize that incompleteness
is essential in a rational view of life as a whole.
It is not always what people actually accomplish
that most accurately defines them.
It can also be what they are trying to do and be—the
goals for which they aspire,
the hopes and yearnings that are theirs.

✢

Trouble is not necessarily an intruder.
There are times when a detour means
a better road to follow.
Everything will not be perfect in this life, and we
ought not to expect it to be.

One slip doesn't mean we are forever a sinner any
more than one good deed makes us forever a saint.

✦

It is the recognition that all people carry with them
some sorrows and pain that encourages us to be
thoughtful with all.

✦

Laughter is God's hand
on the shoulder of a troubled world.

✦

The reward for a job well done
is being the one who did it.

✦

Adversity teaches many lessons
that we can learn no other way.

✦

No matter how depraved or dissipated humans may
sometimes be, they are still God's children—loved and
accepted. Everyone is someone—someone divine.
It is not what happens to us, but what happens in us,
that supremely counts. Whenever we conquer
our own fears and failures, whenever we do with love
and courage the thing we have to do, then no matter
what the result may seem to be at the moment,
we are victorious and are counted
as those who are successful in the eyes of God.

We are all less than we wish we were. None of us ever arrives. We are always in the process of becoming. But we all need encouragement in the good we do.

Faith

Faith enters our lives when, with humility and courage, we set out to follow the path of love and service, commitment and conviction. It enters when we recognize that by remembering God's gifts, God's sense of order, God's moral, physical and spiritual laws, and God's goodness, we become empowered to meet the problems and sorrows we encounter in our lives. It enters when we can live God's love for each of us so fully that we can find joy in the midst of sadness, kindness in the midst of ill will, and gladness in the midst of discouragement.

We are given only enough glimpses of God and the pattern God is weaving to sustain our faith and make us yearn for the nearer presence and larger knowledge which is eternal life. God does not coerce us into faith, but draws us by love. Through faith the Creator shows us that eternal life begins now for those who live with a consciousness of God's continuous presence.

Contrary to what many believe,
doubt is not the opposite of faith,
it is an element of faith.

❧

Throughout history, human beings have used
"God's will" as the explanation for all things
that happened—good or bad—which they couldn't
explain. They have used it to condemn those things
they did not like, or to promote those things they did
like. It is arrogant to presume that we humans can
always know the will of God.

❧

Often the religious man believes,
not because he finds his faith easy,
but because he finds its opposite incredible.

❧

Heaven begins on earth for those who are unselfish
and caring, who are sensitive to beauty both in nature
and in human life, and who live with a consciousness
of God's continuous presence.

The meaning of the Resurrection is that life in God
is endless and unconquerable. Jesus' way of life is
deathless and God's causes
are never lost causes. There is a kind of life
that is endless on earth and beyond the grave.

※

We should not glibly brand what we do not
understand, what we dislike or what we like
as the will of God. It is important to think of God
aright, for we become like that which we worship.

※

The contribution of a mature religious faith
to the problem of pain and suffering lies not so much
in providing a theory to explain it as in furnishing a
power to surmount it.

※

In looking out beyond the self to God, whose face has
been mirrored clearly in the great prophets,
in Jesus, and in religious leaders of many religions,
millions of people have been rescued from lesser
desires and have lived lives of great personal
satisfaction and helpfulness to others.

※

Eternal life begins not at the moment of physical
death, but at the moment of spiritual rebirth,
the moment of moving from a self-centered life
to a God-centered life.

With a strong hub of faith, we can take a surprising
number of shocks and bumps on the outside rim
without sustaining permanent damage.

✛

A life of faith is a ceaseless, unremitting quest—
a series of rebirths—each leading to a new discovery
and a new birth.

✛

People do not believe in immortality because they
have proved it, but they are forever trying to prove it
because they believe it.

✛

Nothing worthwhile is ever realized without
persistence. God becomes increasingly real when we
practice His presence wherever we are.

✛

It may not be difficult to find God in lovely things,
but sooner or later, all of us come to the place where
we must find Him in a difficult or desperate situation.

✛

The basis of discipleship is not scholarship,
yet scholarship is important. It is better to have no
ideas relating to religious issues
than to entertain ideas that are unworthy.
There is little that is more dangerous
than energized ignorance.

The victory that most of us can win for humanity
will probably not be too glamorous or earth-shaking.
It may simply be faithfulness
in the daily duties that are ours.

༒

The wisest people are those who, although
unrelenting in their quest for answers,
trustingly leave some of the problems
in the hands of God who knows the whole.

༒

Finite and limited minds such as ours cannot
be expected to grasp all the mysteries of an infinite
universe or know the whole of God's plan.

༒

Life on earth is so very brief that many leave it
with hopes and longings unfulfilled and yearnings
unrealized. Their understanding and conduct,
at best, represent only faint and feeble beginnings.
This dissatisfaction of mere earthly life is what
motivates us to an intimation of something beyond.

༒

Humans are inclined to hammer away at God, telling
their own plans and wishes and often reserving little
or no time to listen for and understand the plan
of the Supreme Architect. God does not speak
in an audible voice, but sensitive souls, by listening
in silence, can learn to perceive the Creator's will.

If God were small enough to be fully understood,
God would not be big enough to meet our needs.

✧

It is not impertinence to question doctrines
that seem unwise or untrue. It is a moral
obligation to be as intelligent and informed
in our religion as we can possibly be.

✧

Religion at its best is always a marriage of rational
thinking and sound ethical living. The seekers
are on a continuous quest to discover religious
conclusions that are emotionally satisfying
and intellectually defensible.

✧

The fun of life comes in knowing some useful
purpose yet to be fulfilled. Human life, by its very
nature, needs to be dedicated to something.

✧

Each life must do some exploring of its own. No one
can live on borrowed faith, and life is a series
of rebirths, not just one.

✧

Faith is learning to live with what we do not fully
understand, and faith we must have,
for life is not so simple.

It is a sad illusion if we look upon having a strong
faith as something to be considered casually.
There comes an hour in every life
when everything seems to have fallen apart.
The need for stability and faith at such
an hour is urgent. Genuine sustaining faith
in a time of crisis need not be an illusion.
It comes to those who rest their faith
in God's love and who daily heed the scripture's
counsel: "They who wait upon the Lord shall renew
their strength; they shall mount up
with wings as eagles, they shall run and not be weary,
they shall walk and not faint." Isaiah 40:31

✦

It is a mark of humility and an eagerness to grow
in our faith when we are willing to live
not only on tenets, but on tentatives.

✦

The great message of Christmas for the world is that
God is in it. God did not create the world and then
go away and leave it. We live and move and have our
being in God's presence.

✦

It is wise to recognize that, at best, we can have
only a partial understanding of God.
It requires eternity to know infinity.
But the partialness of our knowing
must not discourage us
in our quest to know God.

There can be no power in the present
if there is no faith in the future.

✦

Reverent agnosticism is not unworthy
in a person of faith. It is wise to admit ignorance
and wait for more light.

✦

Religious exclusiveness and blind patriotism
are enemies of the God who created us all. I can know
God within the confines of my own
communion—but only part of God.

✦

How do we believe in a good and loving God
in a world where evil rages and there is so much
suffering and sorrow? Why some suffer more than
others, we do not pretend to know.
But by recognizing God's gifts, God's sense of order,
God's moral, physical and spiritual laws—
and by faith made strong and firm in remembering
God's goodness—we are empowered to meet
the evils and sorrows we encounter.
There are mysteries that can be made
plain to us, perhaps, only in the
clearer light of another world.

✦

The work of the spirit is never done.
Our spirituality is a process.

The most humble and helpful people are those who
learn to live with what they do not yet understand,
daily trusting the Creator's love and goodness.

+∾+

It is a mark of faith, nobility and courage
to turn a minus into a plus and to discover positive
good in the midst of greatest sorrow.

+∾+

Growth in faith is a continuing process of rebirth
and growth. The tragedy of life is that many die
before they are fully born.

+∾+

We can easily understand and forgive a child
who is afraid of the dark, but the real tragedy
is an adult who is afraid of the light.

+∾+

We are given only enough glimpses of God
and the pattern God is weaving to sustain faith
and make us yearn for that nearer presence
and larger knowledge which is eternal life.

+∾+

Can we follow Jesus today? Yes, we can. It may be
we follow stumblingly and inadequately, but the call
to follow is worth our effort to respond, for to follow
is to discover the deeper joys and greater usefulness
God would have us know.

God has implanted deep within the human soul
the belief in eternal life. To believe
in immortality is the supreme act of faith
in the reasonableness of God.

҂

What do we make, then, of men who are religiously
unorthodox, but in behavior sometimes come close
to saintliness? God is in no way obligated
to live only where people look for God. God often
appears where we least expect to find God—and in the
most unlikely people. The faithful expect God
to do the unexpected and wise men
and women know to look for the Eternal
where others would scarcely think to look.

҂

Work is one way an individual makes a contribution
to our world. It is in work that religious convictions
find expression, that personalities are shaped and
faith is nurtured. Even work that is humble and may
seem relatively unimportant may be a window
through which divine light can shine.

҂

Worship in order to restore the balance of life
and permit the message of God—
which is often unheard in the whirlwind of life,
to be heard in the still, small voice of calm.
People are just as religious whether they make soap
or sermons. All workers who do useful work
with faithfulness and honesty do sacred tasks.

Prayer is not a way of getting God to do
what we want, but a way of putting ourselves in such a
relationship with God that God can do—in, for and
through us—what God wants.

✦

It is really better to have no
opinion of God than one that is unworthy.

✦

In prayer comes the realization
that we are not alone. We are in God's hands.
When we sense more of God's love and care, we rise
above our fears. Our central protection against fear is
faith in the love and goodness of God.

✦

It is not enough simply to believe in God. It is
commitment to the Creator's will
that gives integrity to our faith. Religion is behavior
and not mere belief.

✦

Prayer is the conscious attempt
to become aware of the presence of God.

✦

We need to let the tides of God's love move
into our lives so that we may go forth better able
to cope with life's problems.

The contribution of Christian faith
to the problem of evil has lain not so much
in supplying a theory to explain it as in furnishing
a power to surmount it. And, it gives us faith
that assures us that no matter how adverse conditions
may seem to be, we are always in God's care.

Community

We are born for community; we share, as humans, a common-unity. It is a mark of humility and maturity to know how dependent we are on one another. As we grow in recognition of our interdependence we deepen our gratitude for what others have contributed to our welfare. We also deepen our conviction to serve and to build bridges of understanding, acceptance and love to God's other children. Great minds and great spirits are a community's largest asset because everything we say and do is the length and shadow of our souls. Our influence is determined by the quality of our being. Each one of us is in community with one another and what we do markedly affects all.

No matter how depraved or dissipated humans may sometimes be, they are still God's children—loved and accepted. Everyone is someone—someone divine. No one is perfect, but everyone possesses some good, even lovable traits. This lovability needs to be recognized and fed. One of the greatest gifts we can give to God is to learn to nurture the good in others; to draw all near to one another in love and acceptance of our diversity. The deepest need of the human spirit is for community.

T he memory of the priceless gifts
which have come to us from those of other
generations is in itself a call
to us to make our contributions
to the betterment of the world that is to be.

～

There are countless worthy causes needing support.
In helping to heal the wounds of others,
we are helping to heal our own ills.

～

A divided church that stands for something
is better than a united church that stands for nothing.

～

We must be willing, and even eager, in all of life
to do more than is expected or required,
or we will always be average, mediocre, mundane
human beings. The great personalities of history have
always given more than was expected
or required and they have always been
ready to take less than they deserve.

Even though we may have a host of friends,
we are forced, in a certain sense, to lead a lonely life.
We all have days when we must come to terms
with ourselves.

～

The life of a whole community is sometimes
transformed for good in its ideals and aims by people
who have never thought of themselves in terms of
trying to be an influence or deserving to be an
example. But in the loyalty to their own highest
ideals, they walk steadily and constantly toward the
light of justice, honor and truth, and the shadow
of good influence falls behind them. They attract
rather than compel others toward goodness, luring
them by the appeal of their own integrity and love.

～

When we sit in the radius of greatness and wisdom
there is always the possibility
that some of it may rub off on us.

～

Each generation has its own responsibility and its own
challenge. What already has been accomplished
is but a prelude to that which is yet to be done.

～

In all controversy the call is not to cast the stone of
judgement or condemnation, but to offer
the helping hand of reconciliation.

We can be true friends of others only as we deliberately
set ourselves to see things as others see them, to work
shoulder to shoulder in common enterprise and to
celebrate our differences.

꘎

Greed, which leads to excess, can blind us to the
needs of those who have not. It is possible to have so
much power that we become indifferent to the rights
and claims of others; to have so much health that we
do not understand the sick; to have so many material
goods that we prize possessions more than love and
friendships; and to have so much knowledge that we
become proud and self-sufficient.

꘎

"We must do something" will always solve
more problems than "Something must be done."

꘎

Until we are willing to seek information
from the other side of our social and religious fences,
we cannot begin to lay claim to open-mindedness.

꘎

When we draw closer to one another,
we draw closer to the God who created us all.

꘎

The best way to aid the cause of evil
is for good men and women to do nothing.

No one, no matter how famous, is above
the need for affirmation, approval and
words of gratitude.

+〰+

The world is moved forward not only by the mighty
shoves of the heroes and the intelligentsia,
but also by the tiny pushes of each honest worker.

+〰+

Sensitive and responsible people have long known
that neutrality is an impossible stance in the presence
of any critical issue. If we do not stand
with the oppressed, we make it easier for the aggressor
to win the day and to continue similar acts
of conquest and oppression.

+〰+

It is incumbent on religious people to speak out—
with the humility appropriate to limited vision —
on public issues. But speak they must, or causes held
dear will die by default.

+〰+

Where is God when evil rages?
God revealed great trust in the human family
in granting us freedom—freedom to share in the
process of creation. We are called to community, but
we have often misused our freedom and have prac-
ticed the arts of selfishness, hostility and enmity
to the vast neglect of the arts of love and peace.

Conflict and controversy are inevitable in a world
of thoughtful people. Controversy is not only
inevitable, but it is actually desirable;
without controversy evils may persist indefinitely.

✝✝

Making judgements by censure of others is often
an unconscious attempt to hide our own failings.

✝✝

Not to have an awakened conscience, not to be
sensitive to social evils, not to take part in righting
them, not to be active in promoting, establishing
and doing justice—that is heresy. Christianity
is life before it is a creed.

✝✝

There are heroes who, against all manner of assaults
and disappointments, maintain a steady confidence
in God and a belief in God's goodness. They lift up
our society and do not lean on it. They assume
responsibility for their own lives and try to be helpful
in the lives of others.

✝✝

It will be a day for celebration when
the great religions of the world cease
explaining their differences and begin a search
for elements of the basic unity
which could serve as building blocks for common
action and world accord.

It is better to work for the good
that society was intended to be
than to continually bemoan its shortcomings.

꙰

Our deepest need is for community, and those
of harborous spirit are part of life's healing.

꙰

Anger and all its accompanying moods, including
bad temper, resentment and hostility, can wreck the
health of the body and the mind. They are as likely
to cause disease as a germ. But, anger in the form of
moral indignation may be the necessary edge of
spiritual vitality. Were anger and moral indignation to
die out of the world, society would swiftly rot to
extinction. It is possible to be good—and angry!

꙰

It is a mark of humility and gratitude to be
aware that someone has paid a price for every
good thing that is ours.

꙰

One liability of any age is that we might sleep
through great change, failing to achieve the
new attitudes and actions that new situations
demand. It is a mark of mature society
that it can accept constructive change.
There is no merit in clinging to outmoded
concepts and unaccepted injustices.

Neutrality is impossible. We are either for an idea
or a cause, or we are against it. No one is
an innocent bystander. We are inextricably linked
in one body of humanity. What happens anywhere
happens everywhere, and what happens to anyone
happens to everyone.

༄

We all have a shadow of influence that follows us
wherever we go. For good or ill it falls on others.
Silently, it reaches where we are not aware,
and often touches those we had not intended.

༄

It is a mark of humility and maturity to know how
dependent we are. As we grow in our recognition of
our interdependence we deepen our gratitude
for what others have contributed to our welfare.

༄

Prejudice builds walls of separation.
We were created for community,
and anyone who breaks down walls of
prejudice and alienation and builds bridges
to unify is a great human benefactor.

༄

Most of the great advances for humanity
have been made by small groups
moved by great convictions to do great things.

We can all be gracious receivers and it is as important
to know how to receive a gift as it is to bestow one.

٭

The life of an entire community is sometimes
transformed for good by those who have never
thought of posing as a good influence, but who have
simply gone on living in an elevating way
that others want to follow.

٭

There would be very little love given
if people gave only as much love to their neighbors
as many give to themselves.

٭

The years teach much that the days don't know.
A Christian's "Cross" is not his or her own cross.
It is the voluntary acceptance of another's
burdens, or identification with worthy causes.
The heaviest cross Jesus carried was not the
wooden one He bore to his crucifixion, but
bearing the burdens of the poor, the hungry,
the dispossessed and oppressed.

٭

We need a sense of humor to get along with others.
To be able to laugh at ourselves is a sign of wholeness
and wholesomeness. To see our inconsistencies,
mistakes, tempers and scorn for others
keeps our egos in proper perspective.

We do not serve God or humans in general.
We serve in particular.

No one of us is entire in himself or herself.
Our family and our friends are the rest of us. We
need others to find our own deepest fulfillments.

A society is continuously recreated for good
or ill by its members.

People are not coerced into goodness, they are lured
into it by attractive, radiant and joyful personalities.

What we see in our society depends on what we are
looking for. What we are looking for reveals what we
are. What we are depends on what we think in our
hearts and what we do with our hands.

Triumphant Living

We underrate no religious duty as much as the duty of being joyful. The mark of religious people is gratitude and delight. Joy appears in many forms. It comes to those who respond to God's call for concern for the poor and homeless, or compassion for the rejected sick and for the many victims of prejudice. These persons shall experience the joy that comes from truly living life to the full. It comes to those whose small and countless acts of kindness and caring go unheralded each day, but which are real and helpful to many. These millions of people chose to light a candle rather than curse the darkness. It comes to those whose self-respect, self-discipline, intellectual power and moral growth is found in their work; labor which makes a contribution to our world.

It comes to those who learn that some of life's deepest insights are larger truths ushered into our lives by pain and sorrow and yet who sing most gloriously when assaulted by the winds of adversity. It comes to those who sing, dance and rejoice in the great truths that give life purpose and meaning and enable us to live with dignity and joy, knowing that we are always, in life or death, in God's presence, God's love and God's care.

sometimes think I could get
a lot done if I didn't have so many
other things to do.

The obvious necessity for bringing meaning
to the interruptions and the fragmented bits and
pieces of days and of our lives, is to place them
in a framework constructed of patience, perseverance,
good humor, vision, caring and concern, with just
enough flexibility to notice and perhaps to follow a
new direction some interruption may be leading us.

The characteristics that we admire in human
nature grow best in a soil mixed with trouble.
Without hardship there would be no hardihood.
Without calamity there would be no courage.
Without trouble there would
be no triumphant living.
Many do not endure in the midst of privation
and disappointment; they prevail.

It is a mark of high purpose to desire an intelligent
faith. It is not easy to come by. If we inherit our faith,
borrow it or swallow it without reflection,
it is not ours. Great faith must be fought for.

✧

Humans stay alive by growing—by being born again
over and over each day, leaving behind a lesser being
and striving each day to be better than before.

✧

All strenuous living requires time-outs—
rest stops along the way. It is sometimes smart
to be "caught napping."

✧

No one is only one self; we are many selves.
an important challenge in life, then, is to discover
our best self and nurture it so that it dominates
our life the maximum amount of time.

✧

The smallest good deed
is better than the grandest good intention.

✧

Mental and spiritual stagnation are the hazards
of middle age. It is then we should do as Mark Twain
suggested, "Take out your brain and jump on it.
It gets all caked up."
Why is it that we are so reluctant to change—to grow?

It is not so much that new ideas are painful,
for they are not. It is that old ideas are
seldom false, but have truth,
even great truth. But, the danger lies in the process
of putting all thought and energy
into preserving these values
so that we may miss the infinitely greater riches
that lie hidden in the future.

If we expect a trouble-free existence,
then any interruption of our tranquility
is an intruder to be resented. But if we see
trouble as an inevitable aspect of life,
even a prod to something finer, then it can
be turned to constructive ends.

Laughter is a tranquilizer with no side effects.
It is an instant vacation. Good humor is timeless. It is
like good art; if it is ever good, it is always good.

No matter how long we live, we will all leave more
undone than we have ever been able to accomplish.

Most of us, at one time or another, have wished to be
someone else. And yet God does not want us to be
someone other than the person we are. You were
meant to be yourself at your best.

Unless we do the work for which we were created,
our work will never be done.

✦

Choices are a part of the whole of life.
We live in an unfinished world. We are
continuously shaping our own lives, and the world
in which we live, by the choices we make.

✦

We seldom learn anything
from someone who always agrees with us.

✦

We may be held accountable, not only for our sins,
but for our failures to enjoy all of the legitimate
pleasures of this world.

✦

Few of us have many great days in life.
Most of our days are commonplace and routine.
We live most in the appreciation and enjoyment
of the little joys that come and go
almost unnoticed. It is in appreciating and enjoying
the life that is ours that we live
our prayer of gratitude with God.

✦

It is interesting to note that books often show us
that the original thoughts we thought were ours
are really not very new at all.

Life is not so much a matter of finely spun theories
as it is a matter of concrete tasks and everyday
responsibilities. We act our way
into right thinking more readily
than we think our way into right acting.

+∿+

It is wise to take pleasure in the blessings and skills
of others. When we find someone who surpasses us,
be thankful that such gifts are in our midst,
a public banquet to which we are all invited.
The remedy to envy is to learn to accept one's self
and one's gifts, however modest, and to make
the best use of them to make a better world.

+∿+

God holds us accountable only for what we are
capable of becoming or doing. People are fools
not to be what they can because they can't be what
they think they want to be.

+∿+

The real measure of our wealth is how much we would
be worth if we lost all our money.

+∿+

Character is not a gift. It is a conquest.
And the kingdom of character always lies upstream.
It is never reached by drifting. It comes to those
who courageously battle the currents
and headwinds of temptations.

If our spirits are growing, we experience
new enthusiasm and a deeper appreciation
for even small amenities—a smile, a hug, a handshake,
a meal, a bed, eyes to see, ears to hear,
friends and family to love—the list is endless.

＋〜＋

It is an art to learn how to win graciously
and it is an art, too, to learn how to lose
without being unduly disheartened or discouraged.

＋〜＋

The mature person is honest enough to accept
personal responsibility for his wayward ways, and does
not search for a scapegoat devil to bear the blame.
Whether we think of the devil as a literal person
or a terrifying evil potency, or whether we think
of the devil as a symbolic word for the human tendency
to succumb to the lower trends of our nature will vary
with the individual's training and beliefs. It is really
not the most important thing. The important issue
is: how do we respond in the hour of temptation?

＋〜＋

Courage is the conquest of fear,
rather than the absence of it.

＋〜＋

It is important early in life to learn how to deal
with disappointment and imperfection
and come to terms with our limitations.

Each day does offer its own unique gifts, problems
and opportunities. It is important to live each day
with a positive perspective. It is not wise to pretend
problems do not exist, but it is wisdom to look
beyond the problem to the possibilities that are in it.

✢

If we are to make the most of life we must give
attention to the development of our spirituality.
Enter life with joy and enthusiasm. Step into it
with great expectations. Know that no matter what
happens, be it good or evil, you do not go alone.

✢

Life often presents us with a blank page, and we are at
a loss as to what to put on it. The wisest response is to
keep steadily at the important task at hand and hope
that the story our life tells
will represent our highest possibilities.

✢

At times we must take what yesterday did to us,
or what we did to yesterday, and see what we can make
of it today. We often must concern ourselves
with the remnants of life.

✢

A negative situation is rarely without positive
possibilities provided the loss or imperfection is met
with humility and perspective
and does not kill the spirit of continuing endeavor.

Those who aim to live courageously today must often
be willing to sacrifice momentary satisfactions
and endure relative hardships for the sake of worthy
goals and high causes.

✦

We must learn to let go, and to learn how to hold on.
There should by rhythms in life
as there are rhythms in nature, first stress of toil,
and then happy release from it.

✦

Even after conscientious study, it is no disgrace
to feel that we do not have all of the answers.
We have stopped learning if we do not feel
a little less informed each day.

✦

At the close of our days on earth
the question will not be how much we have,
but how much have we given;
not how much we won,
but how much have we done;
not how much we have saved,
but how much have we sacrificed.

✦

Patience is a quality upon which harmonious
and happy human relations absolutely depend.
A person who lacks it can never hope
to live peacefully with other human beings.

Happiness comes when we know
that we do not necessarily require happiness.

✢

Not only is there wisdom and common sense, but a
large measure of joy and happiness in being patient
and tender with the young; compassionate with the
aged; sympathetic with the striving; and tolerant
with the weak and erring; for sometime in life,
we will have been all of these.

✢

If we start by thinking the ideal is an untroubled life,
then adversity seems a wretched intruder
to be resented. But, if we start by accepting life
as difficult and tragic, then our blessings—the joy,
beauty and love that enrich us—will appear
so marvelous, it will seem a miracle to have them.

✢

Bad habits too weak to be felt
often become too strong to be broken.

✢

Adversity, far from being a mere nuisance
or cruelty, is one of the constituent elements
in all great living. The pain and trouble we
shrink from and try to escape,
when used wisely, often turn out
to be the source of a new dimension to our
character and can add to the joy of living.

49

Eternal life is not a postponed affair
which comes only after death. Eternal life
is a way of living that can begin now.
Jesus taught that those who were willing to live
this life abundantly and fully according to God's
way of life and service could here and now be
joyfully in the presence of the eternal. There is a
way of living here and now that is deathless.

✛

To be a supporter is a special gift from God. May
God bless all supporters—those who stand behind the
scenes and encourage the good in all of us.

✛

I am not immediately impressed when I am told
that a person has the courage of his convictions.
A bigot can have that. The bigger question is, is he
willing to reassess his convictions periodically and
change his mind in the presence of more compelling
logic and common sense?

✛

Our lives are shaped by a series of little thoughts
and activities that make us the persons we become.
Big doors sometimes swing on little hinges.

✛

Failure can have a mellowing effect on our lives.
Those who know the humiliation
of failure are better prepared to forgive others.

The truly beautiful people are those whose lives witness to a strength of character and are therefore spiritually beautiful. They radiate a spiritual loveliness that refuses to be denied. Without knowing it, they strengthen us and make the whole world more beautiful because they dwell within it.

+∿+

A large number of small virtues, carefully cultivated, sacredly guarded and expressed daily, can add up to a life of integrity and usefulness.

+∿+

Being dissatisfied with oneself is the first requisite of progress. Those who believe they have "arrived" believe they have nowhere to go. Some not only have a closed mind to new truth, but they sit on the lid.

+∿+

There are divine compensations for every handicap—spiritual resources to help us not only triumph over handicaps, but also win something that might not have been possible without them.

+∿+

Now and again we need to escape from the inner city canyons where the sky is cut into narrow ribbons, and look upon the larger world that God has made. We need to bathe our eyes in the dew of the morning grass and wash our minds in the perfumes of the fields.

Being wise and loving in distributing our money
is one of life's highest arts, and yet,
one of its most neglected.

✦

Life is a gift to all, but some face it as though
it were a sentence to be served. They die
before they ever fully lived.

✦

Learning how to disagree agreeably is one of life's
highest arts. We are grateful for those
who are willing to hear us out without writing us off.

✦

In reality, we are responsible not only
for what we do, but for what we do not do.
It's possible to take a false step by standing still.

✦

Many people reveal heroism today just in meeting the
challenge of the daily routine. It is often easier
to "mount up with wings as eagles," than it is
to "walk and not faint." (Isaiah 40:31)
Life can become very daily
and it isn't easy to glorify the grind.

✦

Generosity is best assessed not by
how much is given but by how much is left after the
gift has been given.

We must learn to choose between what is primary
and what is secondary; between what is urgent
and what can wait; between what is of great value
and what is of little consequence.

✤

It is wisdom to practice selective procrastination—
putting off indefinitely what we never really
need to do at all.

✤

It is human foible to blame another
in order to escape the realities of self-blame.
We frequently condemn in others our own
temptations and weaknesses.
It has been my observation that those
most generous and merciful in judgements
of the faults of others are those who are most free
from faults themselves.

✤

Sensitive people are aware that the world was not
designed for contentment. They see too much
to challenge them, too much important work
to be done, too many changes to be made.

✤

We are better able to hang on when we let go
occasionally. Ground that lies fallow becomes more
productive as there are rhythms in the lives
of human beings as well as in nature.

We underrate no religious duty as much as the duty of being cheerful. The mark of religious people is joy.

+~+

The world will be here long after we are gone and there is only so much each of us can do. To worry about something we can't help is useless. Life is better and brighter for us and for those around us if we do not burn up needless energy, holding the full weight of our anxieties and worries.

+~+

Superficial optimists are a peril in serious times. But a realistic appraisal of life enables us to be aware of both the evil and the good.

+~+

Countless acts of kindness and caring go unheralded each day, but they are real and helpful to many. Millions of people choose to light a candle rather than curse the darkness.

+~+

A chief source of self-respect, self-discipline, intellectual power and moral growth is to be found in one's work. Religious fidelity can be assessed more realistically and accurately by the manner in which people do their work outside the church. The test of our religion is not only the way we give our money, but the manner in which we earn it.

Salute the marathon runner who covers twenty-six
miles, but reserve the loudest cheers for the man or
woman who stays with life against great odds and does
not quit on the hills. On such durable souls the cam-
eras of heaven are trained. They shall not receive
a perishable wreath, but the greatest prize of all;
the Creator's "well done."

✣

Too many people miss the silver lining
because they expect it to be gold.

✣

The aim of education is not only the accumulation
of facts and information, but the growing
appreciation of values and worth.

✣

Humility and courage are revealed when we are
intolerant of the evils that plague our own lives—
complacency, indifference, selfishness, apathy,
procrastination and a host of other ills
that invade our lives and deny us the fullness
and usefulness our Creator intended.

✣

Even when a sin is not known, it is known
to the transgressor, and it affects the way this person's
life is lived. But the joys and breadth
of possibilities of a full and productive life,
which are available to those not hampered
by misdeeds, are limitless.

To mark spiritual growth there can be questions,
which when answered honestly, give us a sense
of the direction in which we are moving.
Do I have a greater awareness of God? Have I
changed my mind recently? Am I seeking answers
to new questions? Does my life reflect the joy that my
religious faith should bring? Do I live each day
in an attitude of gratitude? Have I overcome
any needless worries? Do I do something
for someone else each day at some cost to myself?
Do I harbor resentment and grudges,
or am I always ready to forgive?
Do I have any unfinished tasks?

+~+

In the presence of problems and perplexities,
no merit exists in adopting an attitude of gloom and
doom. We tend to become like that which we believe
ourselves to be. We never build anything up
by continually tearing it down. We should start with
the realization of the good we already have—see the
problems, but see the possibilities too.

+~+

No good point is served by looking to the past and
regretting its failures—missing the joys
of the present and the possibilities of tomorrow.

+~+

Success is never automatic. Self-discipline
and determination, and above all,
persistence and perseverance are required.

It is unfortunate, if in our hurry to make a living,
we have no time to pause and make a life.

✦

The game of life is much like a game of cards.
We must play what is dealt us,
and the glory consists not so much in winning
as in playing an imperfect hand well.

✦

Not to choose is to choose.

✦

One reason for our inability to achieve simplicity
is that we clutter our lives with more material things
than we actually need. The quest for the simple life
is further deterred by our having built
an altar to energy and made activity our God.
We need time to be still—to sit, to observe, to reflect,
to absorb, to enjoy, to learn, to put off
indefinitely what we never really need to do at all.

✦

Finding a way to live the simple life
is one of life's complications.

✦

Great ability is important.
But God is not so much interested in
our ability as in our availability—the will
to do what we can.

We may long to accomplish great and noble tasks.
But it is possible to do the humble, mundane tasks
of every day as though they were great and noble.

✦

Half of achieving anything
is knowing what we have to give up to get it.

✦

Money is an extension of our own personalities.
The use we make of it determines the ends
our lives will serve.

✦

It is wise and magnanimous to never let any critical
word or malevolent act maneuver us out of the orbit
of unconditional love, acceptance and good will.

✦

How easy it is to give that which costs us nothing.

✦

No one can find greater joy than that which comes
from taking a barren, desolate
and unpromising plot of life and making
something productive and beautiful—
something that would never have been
except for our effort.
If I do ask myself, "why me?" as I am assaulted
by hardship and sorrow, I must also ask, "why me?"
about my blessings.

The greatest of all faults is to be conscious of none.

༜

How rich we are if we know how to receive graciously,
for all of us receive in our lifetime
more than we are ever able to return.

༜

An important challenge is to discover one's best self
and nurture it so that it dominates one's life.

༜

The dilemma of imperfect alternatives confronts us
because we do not live in a static, fixed world.
We are forever growing and changing and we are
finite beings with limited knowledge.
Even the smallest hair casts its shadow

༜

Humility is the foundation of all other virtues.
To be humble is to be teachable.

༜

The entire universe is God's classroom
and we are all called to be continual learners.
The hard truth is we have no right to happiness.
Those who set about to pursue happiness
seldom find it. A person has the highest prospect
for happiness who makes God sovereign in life,
seeks to do the Creator's will, and desires
more to serve than to be served.

We can all be channels through whom God's power
can flow. It is not necessary that we have prestige,
power, position, beauty, or wealth.

∼

The manner in which we handle life's problems
determines the quality of our days. Adversity can
make or break people depending on how
it is directed. Even those who are infirm can minister
greatly to those who nurse and care for them,
through the gift of gratitude, good cheer and a spirit
of optimism and joy.

∼

In a world which sometimes seems to be falling apart,
we need to center our attention
on the eternal things that abide unchanged—truth,
justice, righteousness, love, compassion and courage.
These are like fixed stars.

∼

When we surrender to God's will of divine love,
self-fulfillment and public usefulness is found.
This is what it means to be saved.

∼

A positive personality sees some good
even in compromising situations. The following sign
reads: "Lost dog. Has three legs. Blind in left eye,
missing right ear, tail broken. Answers to LUCKY."

We are not always free to choose what will happen
to us, but we are free to choose what our response
will be. We can respond angrily or we can say, "What
can we find here to be thankful for?" Our attitude
determines whether we are victim or victor.

❧

No amount of piety on the Sabbath
can atone for a crooked deal on Wednesday.

❧

To be able to laugh at ourselves
is a sign of wholeness and wholesomeness.

❧

How we handle the adversities with which we are
confronted determines the quality of our lives.
Adversity is neutral; it can make or break us,
however, depending on how we face and handle it.

❧

To be successful one has to be able to:
Do one's duty even when one is not watched.
Keep at the job until it is finished.
Make use of criticism without letting it whip you.
Bear injustice without retaliating.
See the evil in the world, yet be ready
to believe the best about others.

One of the great reliefs of life
is to discover one's own mediocrity.
Two very important days in every life are
the day we are born and the day when we know
why we were born.

꧁

What we are born with is God's gift to us.
What we do with it is our gift to God and humanity.

꧁

One life can make a difference—and a great
difference. Each day, each one of us leaves behind
a little legacy of helpfulness or harm.

꧁

One way or another, transgressions do come to light.
And although God can forgive the sin,
God cannot remove the consequences.

꧁

All of us must make several important connections
if ours is to be a live and vital life. It is advisable
to keep connections with our own best selves—
with our best physical selves, with our best mental
selves, with the best thoughts and the best books,
with the Bible, with family and friends,
with our work . . . with God who gave us life.

People are never more insecure than when they
become obsessed with their fears at the expense
of their dreams, or when the ability to fight becomes
more important than the things worth fighting for.

Even though everyone wants to live a long time,
nobody wants to be old.

One of the chief challenges confronting all of us
is to stay alive as long as we live.

One of God's greatest gifts—
perhaps the greatest gift—to each of us is being born
into an unfinished world and given a share with God
in creation. We become worthy of this great trust
when we commit our lives to the Creator's way of
unconditional, non-manipulative, all-accepting love.

I may hope that in taking note of the mistakes
of others, I might be wise enough to correct my own.

When we follow duty, we enter into life.
Duty is not our chain, but our release—a release into
competent, joyful and useful living. Duty is
the very condition of abundant living.

Asking for all things that we might enjoy life,
we are given life that we might enjoy all things.

✺

Life is not made up of great sacrifices and duties,
but of little things in which smiles and kindness and
small obligations, given daily, are what win the heart
and reveal what is real and good. Those who inspire
us are the generous souls who pour out their lives
without measuring. They give more than they have to
and take less than they deserve.

✺

The story of history is, in large measure, the story
of men and women who have overcome great odds,
surmounted failures and made a significant
contribution to life even in the presence of defeat.

✺

It is amazing that some otherwise sensible people
have a way of seeing only the problem
and not the promise.

✺

There are no hopeless situations. There are only
those who have grown hopeless about them.
There are always things we can do to make life
brighter and better for others. It may not be
the project for which we had hoped or been trained.
It may seem commonplace and simple,
but it can be very important.

One of life's chief joys is to take an unpromising
situation and work to create something beautiful
where nothing beautiful has ever been.

＋～＋

Greatness is nearby in many people if we have the eyes
to see it. It is unheralded heroes and heroines
who have forsaken their own plans and pleasure
to care for an invalid wife or husband,
parent or child; there are single parents; there are
those who walk on streets who are veterans
of mental health wars; there are those who didn't
quite make it in the corporate race for the roses.
Others dwell in bodies of pain, twisted and deformed
by disease. The world is not devoid of heroes and
heroines; we see them around us every day.
They will not often capture the attention
of the media or be recipients of medals or plaques,
but they deserve to be saluted.

＋～＋

One of the marks of greatness is the ability
to be able to see potential greatness in others.

＋～＋

We tend to measure our success in life
by the wrong yardstick. The question is not so much
what we achieve as what we become. What do both
success and failure do to us? The important thing is
that we have learned through it all
patience, humility, tenderness, compassion
and an utter dependence upon God.

The needed lesson in life is to learn how to meet
and deal with danger—not how to avoid danger.
When we try to carry the responsibilities of a lifetime
all at one moment, it is overpowering and we fail. But
day by day builds a pattern of victory.

+∾+

Those who know no hardships will know
no hardihood. Adversity, far from being a mere
nuisance or cruelty, is one of the constituent
elements in all great living and is to be finely
and constructively used.

+∾+

The salvation of the world depends on men
and women who will take the risk
of facing ill will with goodwill, people who will try
to break the vicious cycle of evil.

+∾+

It is important to know that success
in God's eyes is not what we achieve, but what the
process of the struggle does to us—
not where we are, but what we are.

+∾+

The real heroes in life are those who refuse
to let discouragement defeat them.
In the rush, hurry and tension of life today, it is
important to develop the habit of taking time—of
making time—to be quiet, to listen, be still and grow.

The good life is marked by countless little
extra deeds of love and helpfulness done
throughout each day. When we extend
ourselves and do the extras that are
open to us, we make it a brighter,
better, more loving world.

There is a yearning to rediscover elemental
things—things that are honest and basic to life.

No doubt the pessimist and the optimist eventually
end up in the same place, but the optimist
has more fun getting there.

The greatest sin we can commit against ourselves
is having a good impulse and never acting upon it.

The real measure of life is not our successes but our
goals. And it is not alone what people do that exalt
them, but what they are trying to do.

We cease to grow and our conclusions become fixed
at a point where we cease asking questions.

Reading is one of the most positive ways
to use the mind, and the love of books
is the doorway through which we enter into the purest
and most perfect pleasure God has prepared for us.

An intelligent response to life is to find something
positive in each new day.

We are inspired by people who have the gift
of being able to translate difficult situations
into positive gains—those who turn a negative
into a positive and do not simply grin and bear it,
but do something, which makes them better
than they would otherwise have been.

Love

Amazing and beautiful things can happen when unconditional, active love controls our lives. It is a supreme act of love to break down the walls that separate us from one another and instead offer a helping hand of reconciliation, to humbly plan and work toward a society able to make wise decisions and live with one another in unconditional love and acceptance. When we draw closer to one another we draw closer to the God who created us all. When we can love and live amicably with ourselves we can do the same with our fellows.

Love is the most powerful force on earth. It lifts spirits, kindles hearts, heals wounds and sorrows, empowers the broken, fights evil and calls out for peace and understanding, It brings us near to God, and to one another. Love sees the possibilities in others, love calls into being what is hidden, but nonetheless, real. Goodness may be only at the embryonic state, but love can bring it fully alive. In all of life, be kinder and more loving than necessary.

ove of self is an important teaching
because people cannot live amicably with others
unless they can live amicably with themselves—not the
kind of love that sets self above others,
but the kind of love that appreciates our own best
gifts and determines to make something of them
in order to give the best to others.

✦

The healthiest and most completely whole
and creative human beings are those who know
and practice what it is to give love
in nondemanding, non-manipulative ways.

✦

Love is the active power which enables us
to break through walls that separate us—
the doorway through which the human spirit moves
from solitude to society, from selfishness to service.

✦

The atmosphere of a home is conditioned by spoken
words, and the grave of love is dug with little digs.

Be kinder than necessary.

 ✢

Kind words of commendation comprise the most
decorative of all household furnishings.
It is sad in any home if there are
more complaints than compliments.

 ✢

It is not ours to cast the stone of judgement,
but to offer the helping, healing hand of love
and reconciliation; it is not ours to assign blame,
but to accept responsibility for ourselves and to act
with charity toward others; it is not ours to proceed
self-righteously and vindictively, but to walk humbly,
penitently and searchingly toward the truth
that will truly set us free.

 ✢

Much of modern immorality is not so much badness
as it is confusion over what is right and wrong.
Finding our way through a wilderness of ideas toward
acceptable conduct is not an easy assignment.
God-centered, intelligent, grounded prayer can
bring us wise guidance, as can asking ourselves, "are
the highest interests of love being served in the deci-
sion that I make and the conduct that follows?"

 ✢

No person who is fully whole and caring can look out
at our world through dry eyes.

The ability to evaluate, judge and decide carries with
it a responsibility to do so honestly and with love. It is
easier to be critical than to be correct and it is
difficult to be correct in our judgements,
for people do change.

✦

Tender loving care and affirmation can both prevent
and heal physical disease and lift the human spirit
out of the ruts of mental illness and depression.
Those who practice love's power are lifted
above enmity and vindictiveness. They are set free
from the burden of grudges and hatreds.

✦

Words vocalize thoughts, and the tongue
reveals what the mind is thinking. It is not
easy to bridle the tongue, but there is no
merit in saying everything that comes to mind.
It is wisdom to ask ourselves three questions
before commenting about another: Is it true?
Is it kind? Is it necessary?

✦

Love is the most powerful force in the world.

✦

There are intangible gifts that we can all afford—
the gift of praise and the gift of physical
presence. The two seem so simple and commonplace,
yet they are too often neglected or overlooked.

The prerogative of sympathy and
compassion need not reside only with God.
The sensitive human soul sees beneath the
masks that others wear to hide their loneliness,
despair and depression. Each one of us can heed
the words of the great Scottish writer,
Ian McClaren: "Be kind. Everyone
you meet is carrying a heavy burden."

～

There is the story of a mother who told her children
to divide all people into two classes—friends and
strangers. Friends we love too well to gossip about,
strangers we know too little.

～

The most human thing we have to do in life
is to learn to speak our honest convictions and
feelings and live with the consequences. This is the
first requirement of love and it makes us vulnerable
to others who may ridicule us. But it is important
to be able to give our vulnerability to others.

～

Listening is a strong creative force.
Listening is the language of love. Love permits
a person to think aloud in our presence
without fearing the response of a judgmental
attitude, since listening does not mean we
must agree with all the ideas
another is sharing.

We are encouraged to be forgiving
for there is much for which we need to be forgiven.

+~+

Hatred can be like an acid that does more damage
to the vessel in which it is stored than to the object
on which it is poured.

+~+

There are those who do respond to God's call to let
down their nets into deep waters of concern
for the poor and homeless, or compassion for the
rejected sick and dying and for the many victims of
prejudice. They shall experience the joy that comes
from truly living life to the full.

+~+

Jesus never said, "worship me," but he often said,
"follow me"—follow me in the way of justice,
love and kindness.

+~+

Perhaps because the word "thanks" is so small
is why it is so often overlooked or considered
unimportant by so many.

+~+

Jesus was a kind and loving friend to all. He never
met an unimportant person. He wrapped the blanket
of compassion around the poor and dispossessed.
People came to Him with their burdens and left
with a new and vital faith in themselves and in God.

The light of God's love can shine through
each individual's life at the point where that life
is lived and that work done, no matter how great
or insignificant the task may be.

+~+

The highest art of a human's life is the ability
to empathize with the joys and sorrows of others.

+~+

Jesus taught that God's love is as international
as the sun and as all-encompassing as the rain that
falls on the just and the unjust. It knows no
boundaries of race, class or nationality.

+~+

We cannot be certain that others will respond to us
in love—that we cannot control. But we do have the
power to love, and in that loving we can find deep
fulfillment, even if love is rejected.

+~+

Words are gifts, too; gentle words fall lightly
but bear much weight.

+~+

Kindness has great transforming power. Outward
appearances are often deceiving. A smiling person
may be nursing a deep hurt. Be kind.
The deepest need is to be loved, the greatest thing
we can do for another is to love that person.

Each of us has to live with himself or herself every day
and so it is essential to furnish the mind
in a way that will assure a mind filled
with positive and loving thoughts.

✦

We discover who we are when we
commit our lives to God and live God's way of
unconditional love for all.

✦

No one is perfect, but everyone possesses some good,
even lovable traits. This lovability
needs to be recognized and fed.

✦

Those who love are lifted above enmity
and vindictiveness. They are set free
from the burden of grudges and hatreds.

✦

We can never be sure what effect our prayers have
on others, but we do know what our prayers
for others do for us. Our ties of love with them are
strengthened, we feel closer to them
and become more caring.

✦

Love is the doorway through which the human soul
passes from selfishness to service, from solitude and
loneliness to kinship with all humankind.

There is magic in a word of praise.

✦

It is love that sees the possibilities in others. Love
calls into being what is hidden, but nonetheless real.
Goodness may be only in the embryonic stage,
but love can bring it fully alive. There is goodness
in everyone. It remains only to be discovered.

✦

It is incongruous to hold malice in our hearts
when we are on our knees, praying.

✦

People may not be greatly swayed by our thoughts,
but they can be deeply moved by our thoughtfulness.

✦

Ours is a day when the simplicities
of love and caring must come center stage.
Everywhere in our society people are bleeding
to death spiritually and emotionally.
The tourniquet of love and caring must be applied.

✦

There are many people in our world today who are
hurting, plagued with physical or mental ills, marital
incompatibilities, financial problems,
or one or more of the many problems that afflict
human beings. They need to know that someone
cares about them. They need to hear our love.

Love is expressed by overlooking
the faults or mistakes of another.
The message that God attached to Jesus' invincible
life is: "to anybody who discovers this,
I love you."

Sometimes when I consider the
tremendous consequences that follow
from little things—a chance word, a letter, a call,
a tap on the shoulder—I am tempted to think
there are no little things. The good life is the
computation of many littles—acts of honor,
kindness, thoughtfulness and love.
For a life can be made or broken
by such as these—little things.

Reaching Out

Christianity is not merely a creed; it is an action. When one shares in the love, gratitude, joyfulness, community and strength that comes from one's faith it is not possible to retain this goodness without returning to the world thankfulness for these gifts. Reaching out to others becomes a way of life. We come to know in our hearts the truth and wisdom behind the words, "Be kind. Everyone you meet is carrying a heavy burden."

In following this way of life, we seek ways to serve, to empathize, to protect, to nurture others. Our lives contain more patience, perseverance and power. The possibilities for helpfulness seem endless as we grow in our faith and faithfulness. Each day brings new opportunities to express love, forgiveness and an attitude of cheerfulness. The opportunity to do good is always close at hand. Each moment provides us with the choice of finding a way of demonstrating God's love for all His children. "God has no hands but our hands to do His will each day," becomes our hallmark.

f we are honest with ourselves, we
will admit that we all hold prejudices.
We are not born with prejudices;
we acquire themfrom the
family and the society in which we live.
Those who see the fallacy of prejudice
make ours a brighter, better, and more
just and loving world.

✦

The ability to transmute a hindrance into a positive
end is one of the most beneficient gifts of God
and one of the greatest of all human
achievements. We are strong when we can make
our weakness our strength.

✦

Why, in a world that cries for unity, must we go on
stressing the differences, and leave unexpressed
the countless ways we could join hand-in-hand
to bring in the day of justice, order and peace
for which we all yearn?

We often condemn most violently in others those sins
which we should like to have committed ourselves.

⤫

We give to others not only what we have and know,
but what we are.

⤫

We must guard ourselves against the poverty
of the mind that will not think,
the poverty of the heart that will not feel,
the poverty of the ears that will not hear and the eyes
that will not see. Those who awaken us to life's larger
joys are among our greatest benefactors.

⤫

It is a mark of maturity not to be
angered when another's interpretation
is not our own. Humble people do not
presume they have all the answers.
It is arrogant to expect others to share
all our conclusions.

⤫

In Matthew 7:1-2, when
Jesus said, "Judge not, that you be not judged,"
he was alluding to the fact that every time
we judge someone or something, we are also
making a judgement on ourselves.
When we criticize a comment or an action
of another, we reveal who and what we are.

It is common sense to know that it is not always
possible to live amiably with everyone, nor is it wise.
The only people who agree with everyone
are those who have no ideas of their own.

＋～＋

I have never seen a difference of opinion
as an occasion for estrangement.

＋～＋

There is something of great integrity
and common sense in the willingness to work
with those with whom we do not always agree.
The mellowing and maturing effect that can come
when we suffer may make us better able to help others.

＋～＋

To listen to another is to affirm that person,
and to enhance his or her sense of self-worth.

＋～＋

People know that the one thing we have in common
is that we are all different. Lovers of liberty
must expect and even urge diversity.

＋～＋

The call, then, is not to less loyalty to our own faith,
but openness to all—a willingness to listen and learn
from others. It is not to point the finger
of judgement but to extend the hand of friendship
and the arms of love.

It is a distortion of truth and justice
if we fail to be conscious of a person's virtues,
no matter how great the blot.

✦

Courage is mercy and forgiveness
when revenge would be sweet and timely
and would teach the other fellow a lesson.

✦

A compliment is a gift not to be thrown away
carelessly unless you want to hurt the giver.
When someone gives you a compliment,
don't disagree or minimize what he says,
for words are gifts, too. Accept them gratefully,
even though you don't believe you deserve them.

✦

In a world of great diversity, there is one thing
we all have in common. Each of us has a handicap
of one kind or another. One has this handicap, and
one that. The race of life is run in fetters. We are
inspired and heartened by those who deal
with this human predicament in creative and
courageous ways, turning a minus into a plus and a
disadvantage into an advantage.

✦

If we listen, we open the door to the possibility
of learning something new. When we speak,
we hear only what we already know.

There is great integrity and common sense
in the willingness to meet with and share in common
venture of service with those
with whom we do not always agree.

✦

It is as important to acknowledge a favor
as it is to bestow one.

✦

Not all who hear have learned to listen.

✦

Prejudices and misunderstandings are often
dissipated when we venture into the home territory
of another person. Blessed are those who know these
joys, for they shall be continual learners.

✦

Prayer is a two way street. We can hear God
answer that there are things that we can do.
There are ways to share. The best way
to make glad the heart
of the Heavenly Father is to do something
for one of his other children.

✦

Education at its best means liberality of thought
and broadness of view. Above all, it teaches us
to love and to respect the rights of others,
and to make the world safe for diversity.

Happiness is the interest that
comes from investing in a life of unselfishness
and service.

꜀ꙮ꜀

Prejudice damages both the soul of the prejudiced
and the one against whom the prejudice is directed.

꜀ꙮ꜀

Taking risks in sharing our convictions
and the controversy that might ensue can be creative.
But, controversy is not creative if it degenerates
into estrangement, vindictiveness or hatred.

꜀ꙮ꜀

In the presence of difference of conclusion,
it is mature to offer the helping hand of reconciliation,
to humbly plan and work toward wiser decisions and
unconditional love and acceptance.

꜀ꙮ꜀

Revenge degrades all who tolerate its presence
in their minds and hearts. A vengeful spirit should be
condemned not only because it can lead
to harming the offender, but because it also harms
the one who harbors the grudge.

꜀ꙮ꜀

In a world that so readily lauds the "go-getter,"
it is the "go-giver" who most positively
influences our lives.

We may not have people knocking on our door
for shelter, but there are those who are hoping we will
invite them out of a rough and troubling sea
into our harbor of friendship.

✦

Each task that contributes to human good is sacred
work. No helpful vocation is more sacred
than another. All service ranks the same with God.

✦

The virus of prejudice that plagues and weakens
our culture will not die of itself. It must be
continually subjected to the great light
of the oneness of humanity.

✦

Hearts often pine away in secret
for want of kindness and encouragement.

✦

Man's inhumanity to man makes countless thousands
mourn. The challenge is to conduct ourselves
so that we are part of the answer
and not part of the problem.

✦

We cannot be sure whether our prayers have any effect
on those with whom we differ, but we do know
that our prayers can drive animosities from our own
lives and bring inner peace.

The world lies in proportion to the number
of ordinary people who have such intense pride and
love for themselves that they will permit
in themselves no bigotry, prejudice or dishonor.
They will not permit a lesser self to lay claim
to the only life they have to live.

❧

You can't touch a sugared doughnut
without getting some sugar on your fingers;
therefore, it leaves a trail of sweetness wherever it
goes. It would be a better world if somehow we could
be like sugared doughnuts—leaving a trail
of flavorful joy and fragrance behind us. Wouldn't it
be great if everyone who had contact with us felt a
little happier because their lives had touched ours?

❧

People may not be greatly swayed by our thoughts,
but they can be deeply moved by our thoughtfulness.

❧

Were moral indignation to die out of the world,
society would swiftly rot to extinction.

❧

Do something each day for someone else
at some cost to yourself.

❧

Argument is the longest distance between two points.

Sensitive persons are open to truth regardless
of its origin or source.

✦

People can achieve meaning in their lives
only if they have made a commitment
to the development of their own highest possibilities,
a commitment to loved ones and a commitment
to the divine power beyond themselves.

✦

It is the spirit of love and acceptance of diversity
that must be nurtured. Such a spirit, tolerant,
gracious and charitable, offers a basis for happy
and harmonious community life. Barriers that
separate people must be fashioned into bridges.
Enemies must become friends.

✦

No religion has all the truth. We have
much to learn from one another.

✦

Little things are heroic because so many fail to do them.

✦

We give evidence of compassion and sensitivity when
we strive to see beneath the masks others wear to hide
their hurt. What better use of our lives could there be
than to bring light and hope into a world that for so
many people is dark and hopeless.

Often those who do the most good are those who,
like a fully laden apple tree, are so rich in their own
spiritual fruitage that no one can brush against them
without bringing down something good to eat.

✿

Those who can change the focus of their
concentration from themselves to others, losing
themselves in seeking the well-being
and happiness of others, may without knowing it,
do something of great value and importance
for themselves. They compensate for their problems
by forgetting themselves and discover
the profound truth that "whosoever will save his life
shall lose it and whosoever will lose his life
shall find it." (Mark 8:35)

✿

To affirm the goodness we see in others
breaks down alienation and makes firm friendships.
The gift of affirmation or praise is one of the best
gifts we can give to another.

✿

Good friends are real joys of life. Reaching out
to others can become a way of life. People are lonely
when they build walls instead of bridges.

✿